✓ ✗

 **W9-AFP-206**

96-10137

My First Book of Proverbs

Mi Primer Libro de Dichos

96-10137

Ralfka Gonzalez
Ana Ruiz

introduction By Sandra Cisneros

CHILDREN'S BOOK PRESS
EMERYVILLE, CALIFORNIA

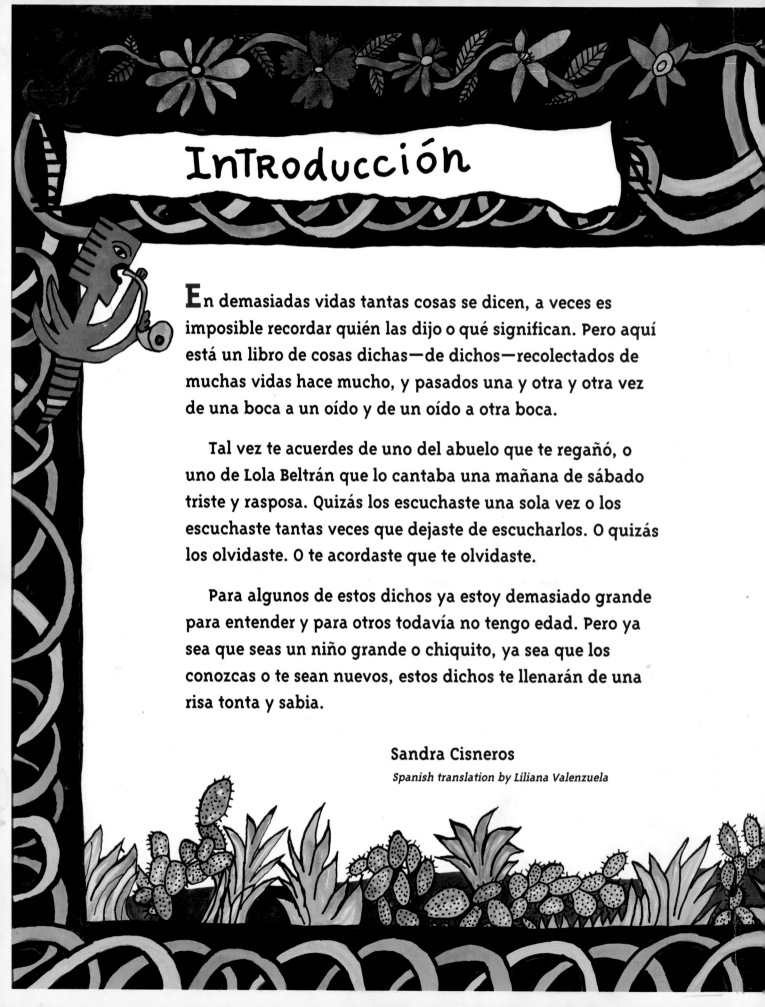

InTroducción

En demasiadas vidas tantas cosas se dicen, a veces es imposible recordar quién las dijo o qué significan. Pero aquí está un libro de cosas dichas—de dichos—recolectados de muchas vidas hace mucho, y pasados una y otra y otra vez de una boca a un oído y de un oído a otra boca.

Tal vez te acuerdes de uno del abuelo que te regañó, o uno de Lola Beltrán que lo cantaba una mañana de sábado triste y rasposa. Quizás los escuchaste una sola vez o los escuchaste tantas veces que dejaste de escucharlos. O quizás los olvidaste. O te acordaste que te olvidaste.

Para algunos de estos dichos ya estoy demasiado grande para entender y para otros todavía no tengo edad. Pero ya sea que seas un niño grande o chiquito, ya sea que los conozcas o te sean nuevos, estos dichos te llenarán de una risa tonta y sabia.

Sandra Cisneros
Spanish translation by Liliana Valenzuela

Introduction

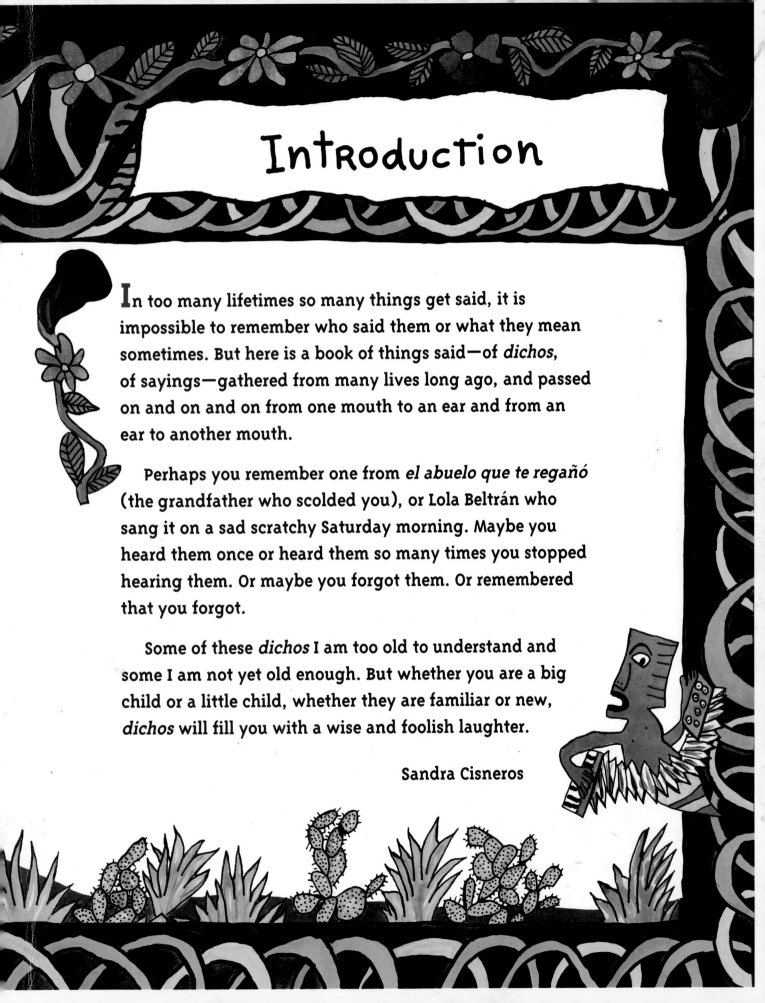

In too many lifetimes so many things get said, it is impossible to remember who said them or what they mean sometimes. But here is a book of things said—of *dichos*, of sayings—gathered from many lives long ago, and passed on and on and on from one mouth to an ear and from an ear to another mouth.

Perhaps you remember one from *el abuelo que te regañó* (the grandfather who scolded you), or Lola Beltrán who sang it on a sad scratchy Saturday morning. Maybe you heard them once or heard them so many times you stopped hearing them. Or maybe you forgot them. Or remembered that you forgot.

Some of these *dichos* I am too old to understand and some I am not yet old enough. But whether you are a big child or a little child, whether they are familiar or new, *dichos* will fill you with a wise and foolish laughter.

Sandra Cisneros

La Experiencia es La Mamá de La Ciencia

Experience is the Mama of Science

EL QUE no monta no CAE

if you don't RIDE, you can't fall

El que es buen gallo
dondequiera Canta

a good ROOSTER can CROW anywhere

a fuerza ni Los Zapatos Entran

WHEN YOU USE FORCE, NOT EVEN YOUR SHOES fit

FROM the plate to the mouth
the soup sometimes spills

Sing EVERY day and chase

About my First Book of Proverbs

Dichos are like the kisses of language. There is one for each occasion and they appear to remind us that we are not alone; sometime, somewhere, someone has already lived the same situation and said something similar about it. —*Ana Ruiz*

RALFKA GONZALEZ is a self-taught artist whose work creates an important bridge between folk art tradition and contemporary art. Born in San Antonio, Texas, he now lives in San Francisco, California.

ANA RUIZ is a self-taught painter, writer, and sculptor. She has also designed theater sets and organized art workshops for young people. Born in Barcelona, Spain, she now lives in San Francisco, California.

Pictures and text copyright © 1995 by Ralfka Gonzalez and Ana Ruiz. All rights reserved.
Introduction copyright © 1995 by Sandra Cisneros, printed by permission
   of Susan Bergholz Literary Services, New York.
Spanish translation of the Introduction copyright © 1995 by Children's Book Press.

Editor: Harriet Rohmer   Consulting Editor: Francisco X. Alarcón
Art Direction: Mira Reisberg   Design and Production: Katherine Tillotson

Children's Book Press is the pioneer publisher of multicultural and bilingual literature
for children—since 1975. Write us for a complimentary catalog:
Children's Book Press, 6400 Hollis Street, Suite 4, Emeryville, CA 94608.

Library of Congress Cataloging-in-Publication Data
Gonzalez, Ralfka.
My first book of proverbs = Mi primer libro de dichos / Ralfka Gonzalez and Ana Ruiz:
introduction by Sandra Cisneros. p. cm.
Summary: Humorous contemporary illustrations of traditional Mexican American proverbs,
which appear in both English and Spanish. ISBN 0-89239-134-0
1. Proverbs—Juvenile literature. 2. Mexican American proverbs—Juvenile literature.
[1. Proverbs. 2. Spanish language materials—Bilingual.] I. Ruiz, Ana. II. Title.
PN6405.G66 1995   398.9'61'0896872073—dc20   95-7588 CIP AC

Printed in China through Marwin Productions
10 9 8 7 6 5 4 3 2 1

Dedications
Special thanks to my family and friends; to Judith Stein, H.D. Ivey, and Cecilia Sánchez Duarte.—R.G.
For Mario Patiño, who showed me the way of color; for J.P. forever; for Calico; and, of course, the Interior Circle.—A.R.
And for all the people who told us we would never be able to live our big dream.—R.G. and A.R.